YOU'VE GRADUATED
NOW WHAT?
10 STEPS TO STAND OUT AND GET HIRED IN THE NEW ECONOMY

Monica D. Allen   E. K. Allen

You've Graduated... Now What?

Copyright © 2012 by Monica D. Allen and E. K. Allen.

All rights reserved. No part of this book may be used or reproduced in any manner whatsoever without written permission from the authors.

FIRST EDITION 2012

Print Edition ISBN: 978-0-9856056-0-5
EPUB Edition ISBN: 978-0-9856056-1-2
MOBI Edition ISBN: 978-0-9856056-2-9

DEDICATION FROM MONICA D. ALLEN

To my grandmother, Ola Mae Jackson. The work ethic she displayed each and every day of her life has shaped me to be the person I am today. She taught me to be on time and to always work as if someone is watching...do not be a slacker, do not burn bridges and treat people the way you would like to be treated.

DEDICATION FROM E. K. ALLEN

This book is dedicated to my beautiful daughter Imana. Hard work, steadfastness, and some sleepless nights will be required to be successful. Do not look for handouts. Ultimately you create your own success. Do not let anyone or anything hold you back.

ABOUT THE AUTHORS

E. K. Allen and Monica Allen are the co-founders of APGG, a multi-brand creative services firm in Atlanta, Georgia. The APGG brands include stuff4GREEKS.com, an Internet retailer of custom fraternity and sorority paraphernalia; Zeus' Closet custom clothing stores; Monica Allen Interiors, and E. K. Allen Creative, a corporate image design studio with notable clients such as Tyler Perry.

CONTENTS

1. Get Your Résumé Right 12
   - Spelling and grammar must be perfect 12
   - The cover letter 13
   - Do not use text talk 15
   - Tell the truth…It will come out eventually 15
   - The employer is thinking: "WIIFM?" 16
   - Create different versions of your résumé for different jobs 17
   - Managing multiple versions of your résumé 19
   - Keep it short and concise 19
   - Inside the mind of an employer scanning your résumé 20
   - How to layout your résumé 23
   - Other résumé basics: 25
   - Sample résumé reviews 27
   - Discrimination: what employers will never tell you 33

2. The Search Begins 36
   - Use Your Resources 36
   - Campus resources 36
   - Your network 37
   - Online sites 37
   - Newspaper 37
   - The company's website 37
   - Go to the company 37
   - Use your social network 38
   - Attend career fairs 38

3. Applying for a position 39
   - Before you apply to any job 39
   - Read the job posting carefully 40
   - Follow ALL instructions 41
   - Salary range 42

4. Preparing for the Interview 43
   - Get your wardrobe together 43
   - Research the company thoroughly 45

5	The Interview	49

Arrive on time (not too early) 49
Turn your cell phone off or better yet leave it in the car. 50
Be nice to the receptionist and anyone else you meet 50
Ask for the person you have been corresponding with by name 51
Stand, look them in the eye, and give them a firm handshake 51
Wait until they offer you a seat or they sit 51
Answer the questions, don't be vague 51
Speak clearly…do not mumble, speak loudly, sit up straight......... 53
Never speak negatively about your current or former employer 53
Know the appropriate and inappropriate questions
to ask during an interview 53
Good questions to ask (always ask a question) 54
Questions you should never ask 55
Memorable interview moments: 56

6	After the Interview	60

Send a thank you note.. 60
Follow-up 61

7	The Offer	65

What to Expect 65
Negotiating salary 66
Thinking it over.. 67

8	Your First Day	68

You are still interviewing 68
Come prepared to complete your legal paperwork 70
You should take notes.. 70

9	No one owes you anything	72

10	Get an Unpaid Internship	76

No pay?... 76
What do I do as an intern?....................................... 77
Don't be afraid to make your mark 78
The new economy 78

FOREWORD

Friday. 5:00 a.m.
Nearly two years after my college graduation.

My black sweat pants and t-shirt reeked of garbage, stale beer and cigarette smoke. As I drove home reflecting on my life, I realized that these odors had probably seeped into the cloth seats of my 1993 Honda Civic by now. I pulled into the parking lot of my apartment complex then walked up the rickety staircase to the two-bedroom, one-bathroom unit that I shared with 4 people. I pulled out the wad of cash that had been growing in my pocket over the past 8 hours and tossed it on my bed. Then I plopped down on the floor and immediately started counting it. Most of it was one-dollar bills—tips that I earned at work, stocking the bar and taking out the trash at a grimy Atlanta strip club. Judging from the size of the knot, it seemed like I had a pretty good night. But I was quickly done counting and much to my dismay, I had only made $65.

I sat there staring at the pile of money, wondering when I would catch a break and land a real job. After all, I had a college degree. Heck, I graduated from a four-year university before I was legally old enough to drink. If I'm so smart, what was I doing taking out garbage?

My diploma hung there smugly on the wall, staring at me like a bad joke. I thought back to my first week of college and recalled one day when I boarded an elevator with some faculty members. They could clearly tell I was a freshman and one of them asked me conversationally, "What's your major?" I replied, "Graphic design."

"Oh, that's great! You'll come out of here and land a job making $80,000 or $90,000 a year! Good for you!"

Well, it didn't quite happen that way—at least not for me. The expectations that society has for college graduates often leave people feeling like they've failed. They make it seem like after college, you will immediately start working in the career that you majored in and that you will be making a good salary from day one. That happened for some of my friends (including Monica Allen, the co-author of this book), but most people that I know struggled to find a job in their field of study right after graduation. So don't feel down on yourself if you graduated several months or even a year ago and you still don't have that dream job or any job at all.

I graduated from a four-year university with an above average GPA. In fact, I completed the four-year program early, at the age of 20, because I came to college as an honor student with advanced credit from high school. After graduation, however, I had no money, no job and no leads.

After a couple of months, I took the job at the strip club taking out the garbage and keeping the bar stocked. I felt ashamed but I worked hard every night. On some nights my former college classmates, the ones who were lucky enough to get good jobs right out of school, would come to the club to party. I was so embarrassed when they saw me taking out the trash and mopping the floor. I had a college degree just like they did but I had to do work that I considered demeaning just to make ends meet. I often wondered, "What is wrong with me?"

Since I worked at night I spent my days applying for jobs, taking more classes, interviewing or doing freelance graphic-design gigs. For two years nothing long-term panned out for me and eventually the club I worked at got shut down. Once again I was unemployed with no job leads.

I didn't understand what I was doing wrong—I did everything that I was taught to do. My mother told me to wear a suit and tie to every interview; I did that. Books told me to keep my résumé succinct and error-free; I did that. I showed up early to interviews, expressed how great I was and explained why they should want to hire me. No luck. I would get freelance gigs here and there but still no job, no career moves.

Finally, one day I said, "To heck with it." On my next interview, I tossed out all of the conventional techniques and did practically the opposite of what I had been doing. We will cover those things in this book.

After a second interview and a skills test, I got the job as senior graphic designer at a well-known newspaper. My degree was in graphic arts, so this job was right up my alley. The schedule was perfect, the pay was good, the work was fulfilling and the people were great!

I worked at the paper for a couple of years and learned a lot in the process. While working there, I started receiving some high-profile visibility for my freelance work. Eventually, I started my own graphic design business and resigned from the newspaper.

Now I'm conducting interviews and sitting on the other side of the desk as the hiring manager bringing in people to work for me. In just a few years, I went from sending out my résumés to sorting through other people's résumés, deciding whether or not to call them in for an interview. Due to the nature of our business and our clientele, most of the people that apply to work at our company happen to be fresh out of college. Therefore, we have become job-search experts for new college grads. Monica and I thoroughly understand the dynamics of the job hunt from the perspectives of both job applicant and hiring executive so we decided to write this book.

Throughout the years I've made good and bad hiring decisions. Now when someone is sitting in front of me in an interview feeding me a bunch of crap, I can almost sense it immediately because just a few years ago, I was sitting on the other side of the desk feeding that same crap to someone else. I now understand exactly what hiring managers want in an employee and why. There are certain things that job candidates do, say and ask that automatically tell me they are not the person we should hire.

In this book I will explain in detail everything that I did wrong when I was searching for a job as well as mistakes that I've witnessed other people make so that you can avoid those same pitfalls. I will also explain what I did right and what I've seen other people do right.

Monica's experience was very different from mine so we have combined our learning points to help guide you in the right direction, step-by-step. Enjoy. Learn. Succeed.

—*E.K. Allen*

Preface

Today's economy has brought about new challenges for recent graduates looking for jobs. Given the current climate it is extremely important to be prepared for what awaits you once you graduate. You must do everything possible to give yourself an edge over the competition and currently, competition is fierce. There are people with lots of experience in the workforce looking for jobs right alongside recent graduates, so the last thing you want is not to be polished in every way and thus hinder yourself from getting the job you desire.

I got my first job right out of college. I always wanted to be a corporate executive wearing nice tailored suits with designer heels and carrying a leather briefcase. I entered Corporate America in the field of insurance. I entered the firm at the bottom of the totem pole in my department. I was determined to learn as much as I could as fast as I could. I advanced fairly quickly by staying on top of my tasks and always looking to the next level to see what else I could take on so that my manager would notice that I was ready for a promotion. After eight years, I left my corporate job to work full-time in a business that my husband and I started a couple of years earlier. Luckily the corporate and now the entrepreneurial experiences have provided me with the unique opportunity to sit on both sides of the desk. I have been the interviewee and now as a business owner I am the interviewer.

Looking back I realize that when I graduated from college I did not have it all figured out. I am sure I made some crucial mistakes that did not get me in the door for an interview or that did not lead to a second interview. Now knowing what I look for as an employer, however, I have an entirely different perspective. I usually have the opportunity of interviewing several people per year for various positions in our company and with each interview process I learn something new. These are the things I want to share with you. I will tell you some dos and don'ts of the job search and interview process. I will also discuss methods for getting yourself in the door for the first interview and to ensure that you are called back for a second. I want to help make your search easier, more productive and ultimately, rewarding. You *can* land your dream job in this new economy.

—Monica

1

Get Your Résumé Right

In most cases, your résumé alone will not get you hired, but it is the first image that a hiring manager has of you. Therefore, it is crucial that you get it right. In the coming pages, we will provide tips and actual samples of good and bad cover letters and résumés. All samples used in this book are real, but the names have been changed to protect people's privacy. Any similarity to actual persons is purely coincidence.

Spelling and grammar must be perfect

Check for grammatical errors and then check again. Get a parent and a friend to check it for you as well.

If you can't get it right on your résumé, then how much stuff would you mess up while working here? That is a question an employer would ask themselves. Your résumé should be clean and easy to read. Use bullet points.

One of the requirements we list on every job posting is that an individual "must be detail-oriented." Receiving a résumé with misspelled words and grammatical errors lets an employer that attention to detail is a skill you lack. You did not even pay attention to something as important as your résumé or cover letter. Every email and résumé that we receive with grammatical errors or misspelled words gets sent to the Trash bin. Often times we do not even get to the meat and potatoes of the résumé because the email or cover letter has errors. We simply DELETE. This may seem a little cruel; however, your overlooked errors tell us that if you are not going to take the time to thoroughly proof your résumé—a reflection of you—then you will not take the time to proof the work you prepare for our company. You are not detail-oriented, a qualification stated on the job posting. You may have all the skills we are looking for but you did not take the time to take care of your résumé. Are you going to take care of the communications you send out for the company? The conclusion we would draw is that you wouldn't.

Additionally, please use spell check. Most programs come with this feature and although the tool will not find every error such as "there" versus "their," it can, however, help reduce the number of mistakes on the front end.

The cover letter

Why cover letters are important:

These days a cover letter, even in the form of an email, can set you apart. In our opinion, this has become a lost practice. Though your résumé tells all about your previous work experience and activities, it does not give insight as to why you think you are right for a particular position. A cover letter is the place for you to do that. You can outline why you think you are best suited for a position and explain to a potential employer what you bring to the table. Your cover letter does not need to be long but it should make an employer want to give you a call.

Here are a few examples of mistakes in cover letters we've received:

#1

> *my name is michael jones ... i am interested in the part time position that you have available. i have enclosed my resume for your perusal. thanks in advance for any consideration that you may give me.*

We should have all learned in grammar school that "I" is always capitalized. Also, sentences begin with capital letters and should have correct punctuation. There are no exceptions to these rules.

#2

> Hi,
>
> I've found you CraigsList posting and I a relly very inerestd. Can you please send me more details?
>
> Thanks!

In the first sentence, the words "am," "really" and "interested" are all misspelled. There is no chance that we would ever hire this person for anything. You might think we're making this stuff up but this was copied and pasted from an actual email from a job applicant!

#3

> Goodmorning! I cam across you ad on craigslist looking for and asstistant. I am very interested in filling this position, I am hardworking, outgoing ,and adomate about anything i pursue.I wouls also lke you to know that i am a proud member of [a national organization that we will not name here]. If you have any questions feel free to contact me via phone 6XX-5XX-0XXX or 4XX-3XX-5XXX.

Several errors are immediately apparent: "Good morning" is usually a two-word greeting; the words "came," "your," "assistant," "adamant," "would" and "like" are misspelled and the applicant uses lowercase I's. Read over your email a few times before you hit 'SEND.' Make sure that words are spelled correctly. Again, use spell check which would have caught many of the errors in the above paragraphs. Even though we know what the applicant is trying to say, misspelled words look really bad when you are applying for a job. Don't use a word if you are unsure of the spelling. Instead, use a substitute that perhaps is simpler but has the same meaning and that you know how to spell.

Here is an example of a good cover letter:

> To whom it may concern:
>
> I am very interested in being considered for the position of Customer Service Manager. As you will see from my résumé, I have many years of experience working in customer service roles. I feel that providing customers with excellent assistance is the cornerstone of success for any company. I pride myself in meeting my clients' needs promptly and effectively. I will bring the same

level of energy and professionalism to your firm that I have brought to every company I have worked for in the past. I look forward to hearing from you and providing you with additional information as to why I am the person to fill this position at your company.

Best regards, Ashley Long

Our thought is if you cannot deliver a well-written, clear and concise cover letter, then you will not be able to communicate with our customers and clients. Calling you in for an interview would be a waste of time. Ensuring that your cover letter or email makes a great first impression is essential in getting the employer to check out your résumé.

Do not use text talk

We all know that texting has become one of the primary ways we communicate with family and friends. It is convenient to be able to send quick, condensed messages via our phones and PDAs but when you are applying for a job, your résumé or cover letter is no place to use these convenient short-form words. Abbreviations such as "u," "ur," "LOL," "dat" and others should be the type of communication you use with your friends, not a potential employer.

Tell the truth…It will come out eventually

If you lie on your résumé, it will at some point be discovered; it may not be during the interview process, rather, it could be revealed after you actually get the job. Lying on your résumé says a lot about your character. After you get the job, you do not want to invite questions about your character. Your employer will wonder if they can trust you with other things, even if you are doing a good job. Employers do not throw away your résumé after you have been hired. It often goes into your employee file and can be referred to at a later date. Therefore, if you say you are adept in something, make sure that's the truth. Those skills may be called on at some point while you are well into your role.

One of our previous employees told us that she was proficient in Excel. After being hired, we asked her to provide us with a spreadsheet detailing a number of items sold. While completing the report, however, she actually counted the numbers in each cell by hand instead of using the 'Sum' function. This is one of the advantages of using Excel in the first place and one of its simplest functions. This occurrence left us thinking in terms of what else she could have lied about and how she may be dishonest in the future. No one wants to have an individual on their staff that they cannot trust. In this particular case, we determined that the working relationship we had with this employee was not ideal and she was asked to move on.

The employer is thinking: "WIIFM?"

Your résumé should paint a clear picture of how you made every company you worked for better. An employer wants to know: "**What's In It For Me? (WIIFM)**" Why should we hire you? What are you going to bring to this company that will be an asset to what we currently do here? Are there specific skills that you will add to the company? These are the things you want to highlight in your cover letter as well as during your interview:

Quantify your accomplishments

1. Use numbers when describing your job responsibilities and career achievements.

2. Use cause and effect. What were the results of what you did? How did it benefit the company?

Bad example: Finished laying out the weekly newspaper faster than the previous person in my position.

Good example: Implemented new systems to reduce weekly production time by 20%, thus enabling management to reduce labor costs by $1200 per month.

As a recent graduate you probably do not have a long job history but use examples of things you accomplished at your part-time positions. What responsibilities did you have? Did you manage others? Perhaps there were things you accomplished in an organization you were a part of in college. For example you may have successfully marketed an event on your campus that resulted in 9% of the student body coming out to participate.

Create different versions of your résumé for different jobs

Myth #1—You should create your résumé and blast it out to as many job postings as you can. By the Law of Averages, someone will eventually hire you.

The Law of Averages (also known as The Law of Large Numbers) is the belief that probability influences all things in the long run and that something will happen simply because it is due to happen. For example, if you flip a coin and it lands on heads 20 times in a row, you might say, "By the Law of Averages, the next flip is going to be tails!" But in reality, the coin has no memory and whatever happened before the next flip has no influence on what will happen next. The odds are still 50/50—no matter what.

Amazingly, some people live by the Law of Averages when sending out their résumés. "If I send my résumé to enough places, the Law of Averages says that someone will eventually hire me." Some people blindly submit a generic résumé to any job that seems to remotely fit. This is the most absurd job-search tactic ever. That's like a hunter wearing a blindfold and shooting multiple shotgun rounds into a forest, hoping that he'll eventually hit a deer. The likelihood of that working is very slim. Even if you do happen to get an interview this way, it likely won't go well because you won't even remember what you applied for. Either that or the job just won't be a good fit for you and you'll be miserable there anyway. No matter how you slice it, the Law of Averages is not the recipe for success.

Instead, your résumé should be fine-tuned and specifically calibrated to each opening. In other words, every résumé you send out should be relevant to that particular job. Carefully craft your résumé to fit each job, just like an expensive tailor measures and crafts each suit specifically for the person who will be wearing it.

Myth #2—List as many different jobs on your résumé as possible because this makes you appear well-rounded.

Most of us have experience in more than one line of work. For example, during your college career you may have worked as a bartender, a bus driver, a waiter, a store clerk, a tennis coach and a web designer. These jobs are all very different so you might think that mentioning all of them on your résumé would make you seem versatile and like a prime candidate. But in reality, it can make you appear scattered and unfocused. As a hiring manager, if I see a résumé with various jobs in various places, I think to myself, "This person seems flighty. They might work here for 3 months then get bored and move to another state, in a completely different line of work. I don't have time to start this hiring process over again 3 months from now. [Delete.]" That submission is moved quickly to the Trash bin.

> Here are some of the random jobs that I had before I landed a real full-time position in my career as a graphic designer. Some of them I worked at the same time or while also attending school full time:
>
> - Furniture mover
> - Greeting card store clerk
> - Toy store clerk
> - Museum security guard
> - Busboy
> - Telemarketer
> - Nightclub bar back
> - Computer technician
> - Freelance photographer
> - Freelance designer
>
> As you can see, this list is very random and many of these jobs are completely unrelated so I should never list all of them on the same résumé. Since I was looking for a job in graphic design, I crafted a version of my credentials that only showed my designer, photographer and computer technician experience. If I were applying for a job as a restaurant manager, however, I would list only the store clerk, busboy and bar back positions. The rest are irrelevant. —*E. K. Allen*

Managing multiple versions of your résumé

You should have multiple versions of your résumé. Here's how to do it:

- Create subfolders in your main résumé folder. It should look something like this:

- Put the position title in the file name. Call it what the employer called it. If they are looking for a basket weaver, send them a résumé saved as *JohnJones_BasketWeaver_2011-08-09.doc*. This allows you to keep track of the exact title of the position you applied for and on what date. It is also a good idea for you to save a copy of the job posting in the relevant folder. If called in for an interview, you can go back and review the position and details of the job description. From there you can begin your research prior to your interview.

Keep it short and concise

Interviewing for a new or open position in any company is just one of the many items a business owner, executive or human resources manager has to do in a given day. Going through tens or hundreds of résumés that are 2 and 3 pages long is just not doable. Most résumés get skimmed at best. There are usually 2-3 key items that people are looking for. Some companies even have programs that automatically scan for these things and if you meet the qualifications, then your résumé will be forwarded on for further review. You should know the position you are applying for and highlight those previous positions, extracurricular activities, or educational background that showcases the skills needed for the open position.

How you can get your résumé down to one page:

- State the relevant positions. While you do not want to have large gaps of time missing in your résumé, you do want to highlight those positions that are pertinent to the role that you want, as previously mentioned. If you had two jobs during a summer and placing both on your résumé is pushing you onto page two, include the job where your day-to-day responsibilities are more in line with the responsibilities of the position for which you are applying.

- Reformat your document by changing the font size—do not go smaller than 11 points.

- Try a different font. The one you use, however, should be easy to read. Times New Roman, Arial or Garamond are generally accepted. Choosing the font is not the area to get creative but some fonts do take up a little less space on a page than others.

Inside the mind of an employer scanning your résumé

As an employer, I have to sort through hundreds of résumés in a short period of time. Obviously, I don't have time to read each one in detail. Here are the things I scan for, in this order (keep in mind that this entire process happens in a matter of seconds):

1. Skill Requirements

a. Let's say the job lists the following skill requirements: Photoshop, Microsoft Word and AutoCAD. As I scan the page, the first thing I look for are those key words. If I see them, then I continue scanning the rest of the résumé.

-OR-

b. If I don't see them, then I immediately press DELETE.

2. Work Experience

a. I see that the candidate has done this exact job before, at a different company. Great! This means she will require very little training. I wonder why she doesn't work there anymore. I'll give her a call and ask about that in the interview.

-OR-

b. This person has absolutely no work experience related to the job. Maybe her education and training is related. I'll check that section next.

3. Education/Training

a. Well, she doesn't have any work experience yet but she has specific training for the job. In fact, this was her major and she took specific core classes that directly relate to the job duties. Wow. She also graduated Magna Cum Laude! I'll definitely give her a call.

-OR-

b. No education in this field and no relevant experience? DELETE.

4. Location

We've made it this far, here's what I'm thinking to myself:

a. "Okay, I like this candidate. What's his address? How close is that to our office? I wonder if the commute will pose a problem. Whew! He lives 15 minutes from our office. That makes things easier. I'll call him in for an interview."

-OR-

b. "Okay, I like this candidate. Where does he live? Uh oh, he lives in another state. He says he's willing to relocate. That's great. But how long before he moves, gets settled in and is able to start work? How will we arrange travel for interviewing and training? That will cost the company money; he better be stellar. I need someone who can start next week. Hmm…I'll put him in the MAYBE folder."

Of course we recognize that for some companies location is irrelevant. This is not the case with our firm currently but for some businesses all communication and colleague-client interaction occur over email, video conference or via phone call. If the company you are interviewing with works this way, you will need to show that you possess the qualities to handle this type of independent work environment.

An employer's résumé review thought process

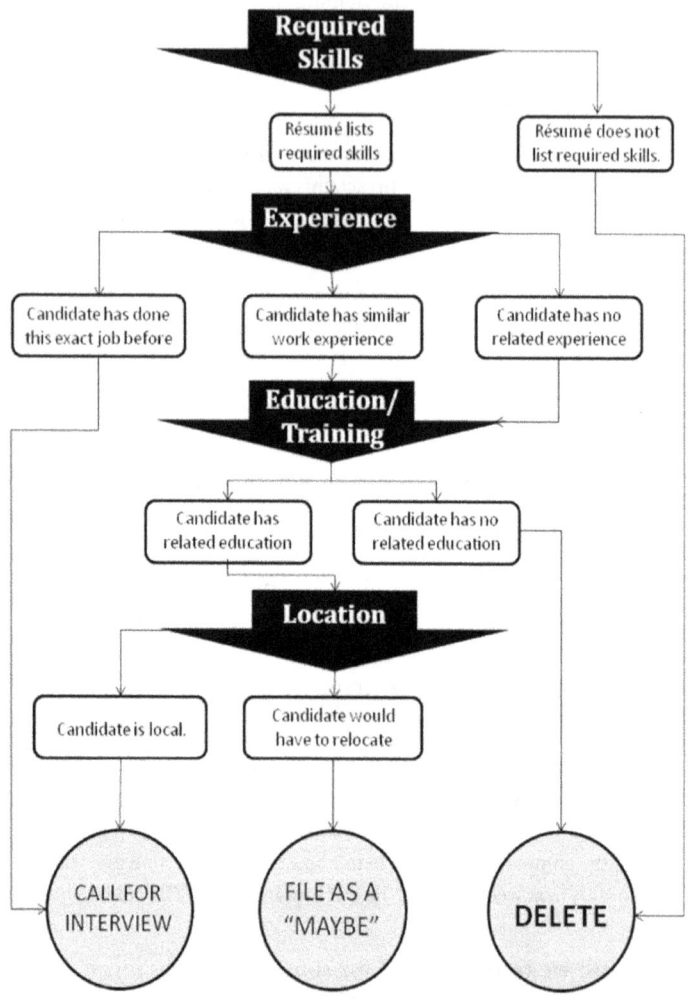

How to layout your résumé

These are the sections of your résumé and what they should contain:

✓ Summary of Qualifications

This should be a bulleted list of your core strengths. An employer should be able to glance at this list and immediately determine that you are someone to consider. This list should contain about 5-to-7 bullet points, half of them being general strengths and the rest being strengths that are specific to the job for which you are applying.

> **Example of Summary Qualifications:**
> - Experienced with startup businesses
> - Learns new software quickly
> - Over 10 years experience in developing web sites

✓ Skills

This should be a list of the skills that you possess which directly pertain to this particular job. If the job is for grooming sheep, there is no need for you to list your skills in rocket science.

> **Note:** When it comes to software, do not include years or version numbers—just list the name of the program. Also, stay away from listing the name of the company that creates the software unless absolutely necessary. Software companies merge, dissolve, buy and sell rights to certain programs. For example, Macromedia once owned the rights to the program Flash, so for many years, it was called Macromedia Flash. But in the early 2000's, Macromedia merged with a competing firm, Adobe, and the program became Adobe Flash. Anyone who still has it listed as "Macromedia Flash" on his résumé appears to be behind the times.

✓ Career Achievements (Work Experience)

You could name this category "Work Experience," like everyone else, but that sounds extremely dull and boring. Plus, potential employers don't want to just know where you've worked, we want to know what you achieved while you were there. More specifically, we want to know what you achieved for that company, not for yourself. So call this section "Career Achievements."

- Begin with your most recent or current job.

- List the dates that you worked at this job. (ex. June 2009-Present or January 2007-April 2010). Note: If you no longer work at this job and you are currently unemployed, your last bullet point should explain the reason that you left.

- RED FLAG: If there is any gap in your employment history, employers will want to know why. Don't leave them guessing. If you don't explain these gaps on your résumé, then it seems like you are hiding something. Any hint of shadiness will lower your score and you may not get a call back. We once interviewed a gentleman for a machine operator position. We'll call him Steve. Steve seemed to be a good candidate because he had 4 years' experience working the exact same machines that we were hiring someone to operate. But on his résumé, there were no jobs listed between the years 1984 and 1999. He did list jobs that he held prior to 1984 and after 1999. We asked what he was doing during this 15-year gap. He said something like he had been working odd freelance jobs here and there, but he didn't name anything specific. We inquired further, but he did not give us a straight answer and the mood in the room started getting a little uncomfortable. So we quickly ended the interview and needless to say, Steve did not get the job. Since we never got a straight answer from Steve, we assumed that he must have been incarcerated for 15 years. This may not have been the case at all. He could have been telling the truth, but we'll never know. The whole thing really just seemed peculiar. If Steve had just included something regarding his freelance position or self-employment on his résumé, there would have never been a question.

✓ Education and Training

If you have very little work experience, this is where your résumé should shine. In fact, if you have never held a job that is even remotely relevant to the position for which you are applying, you should list Education before Career Achievements. It is not necessary to list the years that you attended school. All that does is give the hiring manager clues about your age. Your age can work for or against you depending on the position, the company culture and the preferences of the hiring manager. Note: It is unlawful for an employer to make a hiring decision based on age, but people do it all of the time. See the section *Discrimination: What Employers Will Never Tell You* later in this chapter for more information.

✓ **References Available Upon Request**

Have your reference information already prepared. An employer may ask you for this prior to the interview, during the interview, or immediately following. You will look well-prepared if you already have this information ready to go.

Other résumé basics:

Keep the Summary of Qualifications first but feel free to rearrange the other areas based on your strengths as they pertain to each particular job. For example, if you lack the exact skills that the job demands but you have similar skills that transfer well, you should list those first after the Summary of Qualifications and express how they transfer within your cover letter. If your education is directly relevant to the job, or if you have very little work experience, then list your education first.

✓ **Fonts**

Again keep your fonts simple and legible. There is no need to get fancy with script or cursive fonts. You want to make your résumé easy to read.

✓ **Objective**

This is of course usually at the top of the résumé, however, we have placed it last here because personally, we think the "objective" part on a résumé is useless. It is often vague and doesn't tell you anything. However, if you are going to include an Objective, it shouldn't say what that job can do for you, rather, it should say what you can do for that job.

> *Example:*
>
> Poor *Objective*: To obtain a rewarding position in the field of Graphic Design
>
> Great *Objective*: To bring energy, unique ideas, and creativity to the design assistant position at XYZ Company. (In your cover letter or email you can get into a couple of specifics as to how you plan to do this or how you have done this in your previous positions or activities).

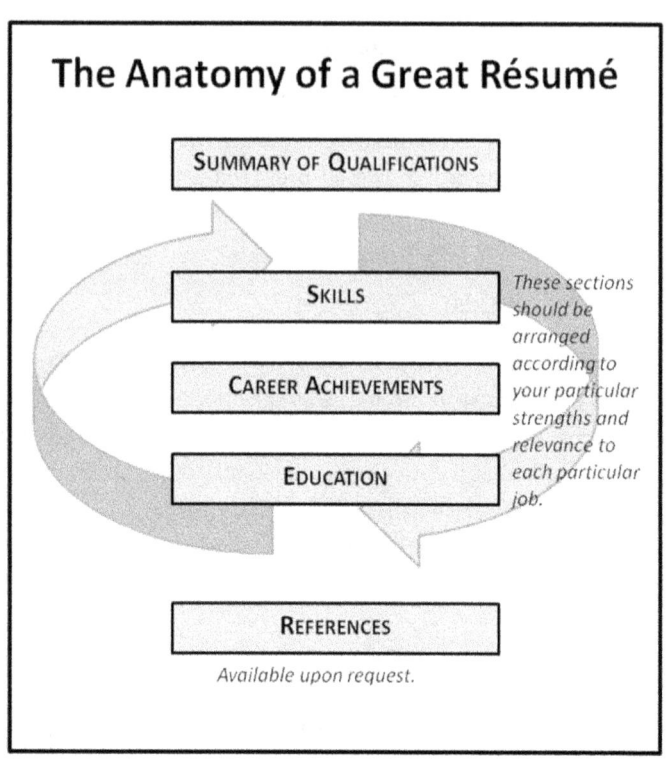

Sample résumé reviews

We have provided a few examples of résumé's below that we will discuss in further detail. Applicants' names and contact information have been changed.

Example résumé #1, page 1:

A. JONES

123 ANYWHERE ST.
ANYWHERE, US 55555
AJONESEMAIL@YAHOO.COM
H: (355) 555-3590

STATEMENT

Exceedingly artistic and versatile Graphic Designer with extensive experience in print, web, multimedia and marketing/advertisement design. Remarkable collaborative and interpersonal skills; vibrant team player with well-developed written and verbal communication abilities. Extremely knowledgeable in vendor and client relations and negotiations; talented at building and maintaining "win-win" partnerships. Passionate and inventive creator of revolutionary marketing strategies and campaigns; accustomed to performing in deadline-driven environments with an emphasis on working within budget requirements.

Skills

- ~Adobe Creative Suite 3 Master Collection
- ~Dreamweaver
- ~Adobe Photoshop
- ~Adobe Flash
- ~Corel Paint Shop Pro
- ~MS Office Suite
- ~Corel Draw
- ~Adobe Acrobat/Reader 8
- ~QuickBooks
- CSS
- HTML/XHTML
- Java
- JavaScript
- SQL
- XML/XSL
- Visual Basic
- IBM DB2
- MySQL
- Oracle
- AIX/Linux/UNIX
- Windows Vista/XP
- MAC

EDUCATION

College Prep W/ Distinction Diploma AUGUST 2003 TO DECEMBER 2005
Campbell High School

Smyrna, Georgia   GPA of 3.275

Ranking: top 30% of class

Graphic Design, Bachelor of Arts & Science JANUARY 2007 TO PRESENT
Herzing University (Online)
Madison, Wisconsin

EXPERIENCE

Lead Graphic Designer DECEMBER 2008 – DECEMBER 2009
Kingdom To America Ministries, Inc
Palm Coast, Florida

Lead designer and developer for web sites and promotional media for small businesses. Utilized contemporary design to create concise web sites for specific client needs. Site creation included use of CSS, HTML, Adobe Flash, online payment features, and form processing. Created and assembled web graphics, including logos and advertisements. Manage a diverse set of projects while under specific time constraints. Creative and capable of designing original pieces.

Example résumé #1, page 2:

Graphic Designer   MAY 2001 – DECEMBER 2008
Georgia Editing Service, LLC
Palm Coast, Florida

Utilize Graphic Design Programs such as Adobe Illustrator CS3, PhotoShop CS3, and InDesign. Work as part of a team to develop knowledge products, create eye catching professional designs for covers and marketing materials. Work with management to develop processes and product development strategies geared towards the continuous improvement of the company. Manage a diverse set of projects while under specific time constraints. Creative and capable of designing original pieces. Ability to thrive in a team structured work environment. Strong problem solving abilities. Ability to work in self-disciplined environment. Well organized with good time management skills. Extreme attention to detail and results orientated. Ability to translate client business needs into successful projects.
Portfolio: www.cachedesignz.com

The above résumé has some great qualities about it but it could use some work:

1. Avoid font shifting.
The résumé shows creativity in its layout which usually works well for a position of graphic designer but since it was sent to us as a Word document, the alignment got shifted and it threw off the whole design. Fonts and their sizes are subject to change based on the viewer's computer. To avoid this, you should save your résumé as a PDF file with fonts embedded, especially if you have very tight formatting or if you are using uncommon fonts. Either that or send a text-only resume.

2. Should be one page.
The length should be reduced to one page. This can be done by reducing the margins and font size.

3. Use bullet points instead of paragraphs.
Bullet points should be used under the section *Statement* and *Experience*. Bullet points are much easier to read and allow an employer to quickly scan your roles and responsibilities from past positions.

4. Include specific examples.

The *Statement* provided sounds good, but as an employer, I want to know what type of vendor client negotiations this person has done in the past and how it helped the company. Did it save the company money? Did he establish a vendor relationship that was not there prior to his arrival? This information should be provided in the *Experience* section of the résumé. With regard to working within budget requirements, how often and what percentage of savings did he obtain on his projects? Again, this information should be provided in the *Experience* section of the résumé. If you are going to include a Statement, it should contain concrete information and not just a bunch of fluff.

Example résumé #2

With the completion of a **Bachelor of Design in Interior Design** and a **minor in Graphic Design Technology**, I have come to appreciate the dynamics of design. Alongside education, I have also learned **customer service** and **leadership** skills while maintaining a job during the majority of my college career. Since design encompasses our lives, the best possible environments are needed to greatly enhance the quality of life. I believe the true beauty of design, whether it is fine arts, graphic design, photography, or interior design, is that great designs can **delight**, **inspire**, **support**, **transform**, and even **heal** lives. With this in mind, I am pursuing a career in design to further this exploration.

SKILLS 1

Skills in Adobe Software (Photoshop, Indesign, Illustrator, and Flash), Microsoft Office (Excel, Power Point, and Word), AutoCAD, Revit, VIZ, Sketchup, Construction Documents, Space Planning, Drafting, and Model Building

EDUCATION 2

UNIVERSITY OF FLORIDA
- Bachelor of Design/ Interior Design, Summa Cum Laude May 2008
- Accredited Program in the College of Design Construction and Planning by the Council of Interior Design Accreditation

PENSACOLA JUNIOR COLLEGE
- Associates of Applied Sciences/ Graphic Design Technology, Magna Cum Laude- December 2004
- Associates of Arts/General Studies, Magna Cum Laude- July 2004

EXPERIENCE 3

DANICA ENTERPRISES, INC./SUBWAY, OCTOBER 2008-APRIL 2009
- Store Manager
- Responsibilities included leadership, **customemr** service, and time management

STARBUCKS, MAY 2006-MAY 2008
- Customer Service
- Barista

JACKSON HEWITT TAX SERVICE, JANUARY 2005-MAY 2005
- Customer Service
- Prepared Personal Income Taxes

MEMORY STATION CAFE/HERSHEY'S ICE CREAM, JULY 2000- DECEMBER 2004
- Began as a waitress and cashier and advanced to Store Manager
- Responsibilities included leadership, customer service, and time management

PROFESSIONAL AFFILIATIONS 4

ALPHA RHO CHI
- Professional National Fraternity for Architecture and the Allied Arts students
- Worthy Clerk for the 2006-2007 academic year

STUDENT MEMBER OF THE AMERICAN SOCIETY OF INTERIOR DESIGNERS/INTERNATIONAL INTERIOR DESIGN ASSOCIATION
- Graphics Chair of UF ASID/IIDA Student Chapter- 2007-2008
- Attended ASID Chapter Weekend- September 2006

ACCOMPLISHMENTS 5

Florida Academic Scholarship
National Dean's List 2001-2005
Pensacola Junior College Scholastic Achievement Award 2004, 2005
Cinno Scholarship for Academic Excellence Award 2007,2008

REFERENCES/ PORTFOLIO 6

Available Upon Request

The layout of this résumé is very easy to read and follow. However, there is a spelling error and the information provided under the *Experience* section is extremely vague. Being that this person is applying for a graphic design assistant position that will also involve a great deal of customer service responsibility, these are the areas he or she needs to highlight within his or her previous experience. What did the customer service role of each position entail from day-to-day—email, phone calls, face-to-face interaction, or all of the above? As store manager, what were the responsibilities? A position of store manager typically carries some form of accountability for store growth and sales. Were these goals met under management? Did this person manage others? Did he or she help reduce turnover? Did this individual develop or enhance a marketing strategy? For example he or she may have started giving out small samples or suggested handing out coupons that led to a 10% growth in sales one weekend.

> Providing specific, numerically-supported statements describing your career accomplishments is the best way to grab an employer's attention.

The applicants below include numbers to support their experience and thereby paint a picture of how they will benefit the company in the position for which they are applying. We pulled these excerpts from different résumés:

XYZ, Inc.
1997-present

Consultant	2003-present
Senior Account Manager	2001-2003
Account Manager	1999-2001
Senior Analyst	1998-1999
Analyst	1997-1998

- Generated $70,000+ in annual revenue by implementing a team sales plan for new clients and new lines of business.
- Developed a retention plan for current clients including appraisal of objectives and services, account receivable collections, study of client profitability, and cross selling opportunities.
- Retained 95% of current client revenues totaling over $500,000 annually
- Acquired a $900,000 revenue account over competitors by effectively marketing our value-added services and team-oriented method of account management.
- Successfully transformed 26% of prospective business into profitable client relationships
- Trained office colleagues to adhere to Marsh's established Professional Standards of Practice and Federal Privacy regulations
- Develop and maintain working relationships with clients and vendors
- Create and present marketing analyses, renewal reports and claims history to clients and prospects on a weekly basis.
- Promptly respond to client needs and resolve day-to-day service issues.

ASSISTANT MANAGER
ABC Grocery,
2005 - 2008

- Supervised and directed a staff of 20 to 25 store employees.
- Recipient of management excellence award.
- Led store to achieve above 80% customer satisfaction rates, representing best performance in district achieving bonus eligibility and earned personal recognition for customer service excellence.
- Accomplished 100 % out of stock targets for Eastern division, achieving bonus eligibility.
- Increased sales by developing in store promotions and effective merchandising displays.
- Managed all aspects of interviewing, hiring, testing, training and evaluation of prospective employees.
- Oversaw proper functioning of major departments in store.
- Managed store close procedures and reconciliation to achieve weekly targets of cash surplus/shortages.
- Completed weekly payroll entries, sales and budget analysis targets.

Information provided on your résumé in this format gives an employer more detail on your level of responsibility and what you brought to the table while you worked in previous roles. It also gives an indicator of what you may bring to their company if you're selected to fill their vacancy.

Discrimination: what employers will never tell you

In addition to the previous filters, employers also look at your résumé for other clues about your lifestyle that may possibly affect your work. This includes marital status, religion, whether you have children and your age. Some employers draw conclusions about you based on this information. Employers are not supposed to make hiring decisions based on these factors but many of them do. This practice is called discrimination and it is illegal—but so is driving 56MPH in a 55MPH speed zone—and people do it all of the time, however, they will never admit it. Unless a potential employer asks you direct questions about these things (which is against the law), it would be difficult for you to prove that they discriminated against you. We'll talk more about illegal interview questions in Chapter 4 but you should know what thoughts may form in an employer's mind if you volunteer private information about yourself.

Things you should never mention in your résumé:

Marital Status

• If you have been married for a long time that shows commitment and stability which looks good to a potential employer. If you are a newlywed woman, however, the person doing the hiring may assume that you'll get pregnant soon and that would cause you to miss work.

• Some employers are hesitant to hire young, single people because they have fewer responsibilities and could be a flight risk, however on the other hand, you may be more dedicated to the position because you have fewer responsibilities.

• Some of these assumptions may sound ridiculous to you but we have included them in this book because it really happens. You should never list or even hint at any of these things in your résumé. Instead, you should do everything in your power to convey that you are stable, dependable and committed to your work, independent of your personal lifestyle.

Children

- If you have young children this could possibly knock your favorability down a few notches. The perception is that people with young children miss work more often and have too many outside distractions. You see, the employer wants your job to be your first priority. The last thing they want to hear is excuses like, "My child is out sick and I don't have a babysitter, so I can't come in," or "I have to leave early because my child got in trouble at school." If you do have young children, don't list anything on your résumé that might give that away.

Age

- Age discrimination is quite common. Depending on the position, the employer may prefer an older person. For another position, they may want someone fresh out of school.

- The stereotypes are that older people aren't as tech savvy and they may be too slow or too stubborn to learn new ways of doing things. On the other hand, older employees are generally thought to be more reliable and willing to stay with a company for a long time. Depending on their experience, an older hire may demand a higher salary than a younger person doing the same job.

- Employers sometimes prefer young hires because they are more impressionable and may more easily adapt to the way things are done. They can also hire younger people for less money. On the other hand, younger people are often thought to not be as dependable. They may leave to go work for another company after a short period of time. They may also have unrealistic expectations of the working world. Some employers would rather not deal with that drama so they might delete your résumé simply based on your age.

- Note: It is easy for the résumé reviewer to figure out your age if you list the years you graduated from high school and college. You do not have to list those years on your résumé and it is unlawful for an interviewer to ask you when you graduated.

Religion

- There are countless ways in which people may discriminate based on religion. Just leave any reference to religion out of your résumé. Period.

Getting your résumé right is essential. Your cover letter and résumé will be the first introduction an employer will have to you. It operates as your ambassador. Since your goal is to make it to the next phase of the interview process, it is vitally important that these elements are concise, memorable and accurate. Make sure you are addressing the needs of the job you are applying for and that your résumé and cover letter are free from errors. This shows that you are serious about the position and that you care about how you are represented. Remember your résumé and cover letter is the first piece of communication that tells the interviewer what you can bring to their company. They are looking for people who will represent them well. Keep in mind that small businesses represent 99.7% of employer firms, so your résumé and cover letter may very well be landing on the desk of the owner, CEO, or president.

2

The Search Begins: Use Your Resources

When you are in search of that first job out of college it is important that you utilize every resource you have available to you. We have listed several below as a starting point but you can be creative; you do not have to limit yourself to just these areas.

Campus resources

We were blessed to go to a university that had a wonderful career center. They had mock interviews, résumé-writing workshops and a wealth of resources, including people you could talk to about your career decisions. Most colleges and universities have some form of help for students and upcoming graduates. Do not sit on the sidelines. Visit these facilities and know what they have to offer. Get to know the people who work in the career center. Let them know what you are looking for so if something comes across their desks, they just may think of you. Many even offer services to alumni. If you have already graduated and are looking for a job, you can go back to your university's career center for assistance.

Your network

Have you created a network? This could be a circle of your peers as well as of individuals currently working in the profession you desire. Internships are helpful for this purpose. Keep in touch with people you meet during your internship. The people you know may be able to help you find the job that is right for you. Also, let friends and family know what you are looking for in respect to a job. What clubs or organizations are you a part of? Were you in a fraternity or sorority? Are you in touch with alumni from your organization or club? If there is someone in a similar profession, they may be able to help you get your résumé to the right person so you don't get lost in the stack with everyone else.

Online sites

In your job search you want to look in the obvious places such as online sites like Monster.com, Careerbuilder.com and Craigslist. These sites are free to use for those looking for a job. Employers pay to post their job openings so you want to make sure you are actively searching these sites and checking them often for new postings and opportunities.

Newspaper

Though the job hunt has primarily moved online, you can still check your local paper to see what job listings are available in your area.

The company's website

If you are interested in working for a specific company, you want to periodically check that company's website. Some companies list current job openings as well as instructions on how to go about applying for a position.

Go to the company

Depending on the type of company, it may be to your advantage to just stop by and see if they are currently hiring. This tactic can work very well for retail-related jobs. You may not want to do this with a firm located in a large high rise building but if you are interested in working in a specific store in a mall or shopping center, it may be to your advantage to just walk in and ask for an application. If you do this though, you should be dressed neatly and present yourself as if you already fit right into the store.

Use your social network

Facebook, Twitter, LinkedIn and many other social networking sites now provide us with another avenue of meeting and connecting with people. It is not a bad idea to let people within your social network know that you are looking for a job and what type of position you are in search of. You may also be able to connect with individuals who are already in the industry you desire to break into. They may not readily know of a job you can apply for but they may be a good mentor or a good sounding board as you pursue your goals.

Attend career fairs

Colleges, cities, even churches are having career fairs these days. You should check as many of them out as possible. Ideally you want to attend those that are targeted to your area of interest. Your school may host career fairs that are all encompassing of many different types of industries or they may be very specific to your major. Whatever the case may be, you should attend as many as possible. Do not take them lightly. Dress appropriately. Go into the fair with the goal of learning, even if the company you really desire to work for is not there. See if one of their competitors is in attendance. Is there information you can garner from them that can provide you the insight you will need to break into the industry?

Making use of each type of resource available to you will give more people an opportunity to know what you are looking to do after college. For example, a friend or family member may get into a conversation with someone in the grocery store or hair salon. That person's company could be hiring for just the job you are looking for but if you failed to communicate your career goals with that friend or family member, they would not think of you. Keep in mind that *you* are your primary marketer.

3

Applying for a position

Before you apply to any job

Present yourself in a professional way.

You may be thinking, "Well I have gotten my résumé proofed. I used spell check and I got a parent or friend to look it over. My résumé is good to go. I have a couple of nice outfits to wear when I go to the interview. I will look the part." There are still a few additional items to handle.

First listen to your voice mail greeting, specifically the message that someone will hear when they call your phone number and you miss the call. Do you have music, background noise or an immature intro that may appeal to your friends but not a future employer? If you do, then change your greeting before you send out your résumé. Again, you will and can be judged by your voice mail. You do not want someone calling to schedule an interview with you to hang up because they hear your less-than-desirable outgoing message.

In addition to voice mail, from what email address is your résumé being sent? It should be something professional. An example of an inappropriate email address is hotgirl101@gmail.com.

An email address that uses your first and last name is ideal. When it comes to reviewing résumés this is easier to remember and find in an inbox full of résumés. First two initials and last name works as well. If you need to include numbers because your name is already taken, that's fine, just make sure even your email address screams, "I am a professional," I am an adult," and "I am ready for the responsibilities of a serious career."

What do your Facebook and Twitter posts say about you? Answer this honestly. If you have scantily clad pictures, immature and negative comments or curse words in every other sentence, a future employer could see this. Employers do Google searches on potential hires. They can find your Facebook page. So our suggestion is to clean it up. Remove those photos from freshman or sophomore year that may not portray you in the best light. Also change your Facebook name if needed.

Read the job posting carefully

It is extremely important that you read the job posting thoroughly.

- Are specific skills required? If you don't have them, don't waste your time applying. Move on to the next listing, however, if you have a very similar expertise, then you could apply and mention how your experience is similar in your cover letter. Whatever you do, never apply without mentioning the required qualification in hopes that the employer doesn't notice. It was included as a requirement in the job listing for a reason.

    For example, if the job listing says, "Required: Must have experience operating a Versa Laser Cutter" and you have no idea what that is, don't waste your time or the employer's time by submitting your résumé.

    If, however, you have experience working an Epilog Laser Cutter but not a Versa, then you should apply and you should mention that in the résumé and cover letter. You should also add that you have researched both machines and you feel confident that you can quickly learn the Versa machine based on your experience with the Epilog.

- What is the true purpose of this job? Companies will list a bunch of skill requirements and job duties but this doesn't give a clear picture as to what the overall purpose of the job is and how it is part of the company's operations. Research the organization and the position as much as you can beyond the job listing. Start with the company website. Your goal is to visualize yourself in the role and try to fully understand how your day-to-day activities would play into the company's overall business objectives.

What not to do:

When sorting through résumés, I set up two folders—Call for Interview and Maybe. Then I simply delete anyone who does not fall into those two categories. Here are some quick ways to get deleted:

> • Ask for more information about the job. I've had people respond to a job posting by sending an email with no résumé attached stating, "This job sounds like it may be a good fit for me. Could you send me some more information about it?" I quickly hit the delete key. Why?
>
>> 1. They didn't follow instructions. I asked for a résumé. I don't want someone who doesn't (or can't) follow instructions working for me.
>>
>> 2. I posted everything that I want you to know about the position. If the listing includes the schedule, duties, requirements, dress code and location, then don't ask any more questions right now. Sometimes businesses intentionally leave out certain details when posting a job to avoid revealing trade secrets or practices that they don't want competitors to know about.
>>
>> 3. Perhaps they didn't read the job posting. We don't hire people who don't read.
>>
>> 4. What is it you want to know? At least be specific. But again, if it's something outside of schedule, duties, requirements, dress code and location and it wasn't mentioned in the listing, there's a reason.

Follow all instructions

Read and follow all instructions when applying for a position.

We often post jobs with very brief but specific instructions for applying. Usually there are 2-to-3 tasks that must be done. For example, attach your résumé, include a link to your portfolio and provide references. Or there may be some additional information required depending on the position. If these steps are not followed, it leads us to question whether you would be able to follow day-to-day instructions and direction. The applicants that do not follow all instructions are automatically moved to the trash bin. When applying for a position, following the instructions given is part of the process that an employer uses to determine who they should call for an interview.

Salary range

If it does not meet your requirements do not apply.

Often times a company will list a salary range for a given position, for example $35K-$42K. If you have no experience and the lower end of the spectrum does not work for you, do not apply. You should not try to make the high end of the salary range when you are fresh out of school or lack many of the skills required.

New Hire Requires Very Little Training = $$$$

New Hire Requires A Lot of Training = $

If the listing does not mention salary, then do your research based on job title and location using resources such as www.salary.com.

—

In conclusion, when applying for a position it is very simple: Read the posting carefully and follow the instructions provided. This will at least keep you in the Inbox and out of the Trash.

4

Preparing for the Interview

Get your wardrobe together

The phrase "dress for success" may be overused but there is truth to this statement. You need to arrive at your interview in the appropriate attire. Researching the company you are interviewing with as well as knowing the industry can help tremendously in dressing appropriately for an interview.

> **Monica's take:**
> I worked in the insurance industry for several years. Insurance was my major in college so I knew that at most firms people dressed very conservatively. We were taught to always wear a suit to the interview, no exceptions. There was no business casual in this industry, especially when it came to the interview process. Men wore a conservative blue, black or gray two-piece suit with a tie that was equally as formal. Women wore a pant or skirt suit in blue, gray, or black as well. For one of my interviews, I wore a nicely tailored red suit. It was a little untraditional but I felt like it looked good on me, showed a little bit of my personality and helped me stand out from the crowd of blue and black suits. The way the suit was tailored made it conservative and I wore dark panty hose and shoes to tone it down a bit.

Now I work in an artistic discipline; our company is a graphic design firm so my expectations are not for a job applicant to come to an interview in a three-piece suit. We do, however, expect a potential candidate to be neat, shirt or blouse tucked in and well-groomed.

There was one candidate that I will never forget. She showed up for the interview looking like she had just stepped out of her garden. Perhaps she forgot about the interview and remembered it just as she was about to plant her tulips. She wore baggy cargo pants, a large sweatshirt that was too big for her and Crocs sandals with socks. In addition, her hair was disheveled and pulled back in a loose ponytail.

Her appearance alone gave me the impression that she did not take this interview seriously. So we had to ask ourselves if she would take her job seriously. We concluded that she probably would not, so we kept it brief and did not call her back for a second interview.

Don't get me wrong, being in an artistic industry you never really know what you are going to get. Creativity in your wardrobe is okay if you have done your research and know the typical attire for the company with which you are interviewing.

We had one candidate show his artistic personality by wearing a pair of nice jeans with a button down shirt, bow tie and colorful tennis shoes. This was a great way to show off his creative flair while still being neat and well-groomed. He was called back for a second interview and got the job.

Again, first impressions are very important. People usually see you before they have had an opportunity to hear you. Presenting yourself in a manner that fits the company is a critical early step to securing the job.

E. K.'s Experience:

My mother used to tell me, "Wear a suit and tie to every interview, no matter what the job is." For two years, I listened to her advice but I never got hired. At the next interview I wore a polo shirt and some slacks. I got the job.

You should research the company culture and dress code for yourself before your interview. How? On the day before your interview, drive to the company, inconspicuously sit in the parking lot and observe. How do the other employees dress? How do customers/clients that visit the company dress? Your goal is to dress in a similar manner to everyone else but just a tad better.

No matter if you are dressed casually, in business casual attire, or in a suit, you should always be neat, well-groomed, clean and crisp. And always smell good.

Don't get me wrong, there are several jobs that warrant wearing a suit to the interview. If you are interviewing for a job in a conservative profession—legal, medical, religious, accounting, sales, finance or insurance, for example—then you should definitely wear a suit. But if it is artistic, creative, outdoors or otherwise informal then you should dress the part.

Research the company thoroughly

Knowing the company you are interviewing with is crucial for two reasons. One, you want to make sure this is an organization you would want to work within and two, you want to go into your interview with some insight on the company's history, mission and vision. This will help you gain clarity on where you can add value to the business's goals.

Ask yourself if you really want to work for the company. Right now the job market is tight so for a lot of people it is just about having a job. One of the things I always tell the people I interview is that we want them to be happy at work. It does me no good if you are miserable every day when you come to the office. You will just make those around you miserable and ultimately, it will negatively affect your attitude and your work. It will also begin to impact the rest of the staff and clients. No one likes to be around a negative or unhappy person as it completely zaps the energy from a room. Thus, it is important for me to know why a candidate wants to work for my company. If you do not know anything about the organization, you cannot answer this question.

The company you work for should align to your moral code and ethics. For example, I would not want to work for a firm that manufactures and sells tobacco products. I know a lot of people who came out of college making a great deal of money working for such companies but this would go against every fiber of my being since my grandmother died of lung cancer after smoking for over 50 years. Due to my personal life events, I could not wake up every day to go to a place that I knew promoted the consumption of nicotine-based products.

Also, researching the company will help you better position yourself to let the interviewer know how you can contribute to the organization. Of course getting a job is important to you but a firm wants to know what you can offer them. Your research may even make you more passionate about the position you are applying for and this enthusiasm will show in your interview.

Additionally, researching the company will help you get your wardrobe in order. It will help you better understand what the company's expectations are for their employees with regard to the dress code. You will then be able to walk into the company on the day of your big interview and already look like you fit right in.

It is also important that you understand what the company's expectations are of their staff as it relates to work-life balance and work conduct—the company's workplace culture. Does this fit your lifestyle? The job may have a flexible schedule but would you be expected to work 60-80 hours per week? Is teleworking allowed? Are you expected to bill a certain number of hours a week per client? The list could go on and on but these are the types of things you should know prior to the interview.

Now that you know why doing your research is so important, let's talk about how you go about doing this research.

1. Visit the company website (s).

> Most companies have a web presence. Review the company's website. What products or services do they offer? Who looks like their target market or typical customer? Are they primarily business to consumer (B to C) or business to business (B to B)? Do they operate internationally or just domestically? Do they have multiple locations or a single location? Who are the top executives—CEO/President, VPs, etc.? Do they show a vision or mission statement? If so review it. Does it fall in line with somewhere you would want to spend a third of your day? Do they seem to be in a growth mode or somewhat stagnant? Are they a public or private company? Approximately how many employees do they have? Do they have several positions open or just a couple? All of these questions and many more can give you a fairly good picture of the company.

If the company you are interviewing with does not have a website, then you should definitely ask why when you have an opportunity to ask questions during the interview. You may also want to make this one of the things you put out there as a special project you would love to take on for them in the future when you become a part of their team.

2. Scour the Internet. See what others are saying.

Start with a Google search about the company. The search results should include the company website as well as other helpful information. Have there been articles written about the firm? If so read them. Were they positive or negative? Articles can tell you about the company's history. They can also tell you whether the company is growing, developing new products, expanding, declining or has had any legal troubles. Are there customer comments out there about their service? These are all good things to know before you enter their doors for the interview.

Also read through the company's recent activity on social networks such as Facebook, Twitter and LinkedIn. Does the company have any videos on YouTube? Researching these avenues will arm you with knowledge so that you can ask insightful questions during the interview. Applicants who ask insightful questions usually stand out because they took time to do research and seem genuinely interested in the company.

3. Ask friends and family their thoughts about the company.

Your friends and family may be able to give you some thoughts on the company. For example, if they have shopped there before, they may know how the staff dresses as well as tell you how they were treated. Did the company leave them feeling like it was a place they would go to again or do business with again? From a marketing perspective you can see what type of messaging they've seen from the company in the past. What is their image of the firm? Is their position effective and consistent?

4. Get to know someone who works there.

This person may be able to give you more insight than the website or Google because they are in the mix every day. They can tell you about the company's culture, work environment and other elements.

It is essential that you are prepared for your interview. I find it extremely discouraging when interviewees have not taken the opportunity to visit our website to understand what it is we do and offer. This tells me that the person is just about getting a *job*, not about continuing a *career* with a dynamic and highly-specialized graphic design firm. Even if you are not all that interested in the firm, if you truly just need a job, you best play the part and get to know the company. Other candidates who do their research will far outshine you during the interview process. They will get the call back and you will not.

5

The Interview

Arrive on time (not too early)

Not sure how many times we need to say this but be on time, be on time, BE ON TIME. Arriving to an interview late really sets a bad tone. It shows a lack of preparation, planning and interest. Potential employers look at everything.

We once had a potential candidate who called us at least 3 times to get clarity on the directions. By the time he arrived he was 15 minutes late and an apology simply does not make up for that very poor first impression.

I realize that large cities can be a bit confusing and cause people to get a little turned around but this is why you should use Google Maps, MapQuest, or a GPS system, and even clarify the location the day before the interview. Use all of these methods if necessary to ensure that you know where you are going. If your schedule permits, go and figure out where the office or location is a day or so prior to the interview.

There is nothing wrong with arriving 10 or 15 minutes early for an interview. This will give you time to go to the restroom or just take a moment to regroup. If you arrive too early, however, the interviewer may not be ready for you yet. They may be finishing up another meeting. If you do get there 30 or more minutes early just relax in your car for a time or pop into a nearby coffee shop so you can arrive 10-15 minutes prior to your interview time.

Turn your cell phone off or better yet leave it in the car

You are not so important that you cannot turn your cell phone off for the hour you will be in your interview. You want to show that this position is important to you. Having your phone on shows that you did not have the forethought to turn it off and focus on the meeting. Also, pausing during the interview process to turn off your ringer is a distraction for the interviewer and can be one for you during what could have been one of your best answers to an interview question. Your answer will get lost during the ringing of the phone and your fumbling to quickly get it silenced.

In addition, the constant "chirp," "bing" or vibrations of your phone from receiving text messages, emails or push notifications is annoying and disruptive. Just turn the device off, or better yet, leave it in the car. All of your missed calls, text messages and notifications will be waiting for you upon your return and you would have been completely focused on the interview and answering the questions asked.

Be nice to the receptionist and anyone else you meet

Many large offices will have a receptionist that will greet you upon your arrival. You need to know exactly who you are interviewing with so you can provide them with this information. You need to greet this person with a pleasant smile and a hello. Never be smug regardless of the position for which you are interviewing—even if it is one level from the CEO. A receptionist's opinion can hold a lot more weight in an organization that you can even imagine. In addition, be cordial to people you meet in the parking lot, elevator, restroom or any location in the building. This may end up being someone you meet with or it may be someone that you are introduced to during the process. Often after you finish your interview and leave, the hiring manager may ask people around the office what they thought of you. Does it seem like you will fit in with the team? You want to make sure they have something nice to say.

Ask for the person you have been corresponding with by name

This was stated earlier but you want to ask for the person you are interviewing with by name. Do not simply say "I am here for an interview." The person you are telling this to may or may not know what is going on. In a large firm there may be several different people giving several different interviews on one day. So be clear: "I am here for a 10:00 interview with Claire Moore."

Stand, look them in the eye, and give them a firm handshake

When the person you are interviewing with comes out to greet you or you are sent back to meet them, make sure you stand up, look them in the eye, say hello and greet them with a firm handshake. People feel like a firm handshake communicates assertiveness and professionalism. We once had a candidate interview with us whose handshake was wet and limp. Now perhaps the dampness was due to nervousness but there was no reason why his handshake was not a firm one.

Wait until they offer you a seat or they sit

If you are interviewing with a more conservative firm, it is best to be a bit more "old school" and wait until you are offered a seat. Also, if your interview is taking place in a conference room, do not sit at the head of the table unless that is the seat you are offered.

Answer the questions, don't be vague

In our interviews, we ask behavioral questions. This means that we expect you to describe *specific* experiences or encounters you have had in the past. It helps us get to know you better and understand your thought process. More often than not, candidates answer these questions in a vague manner. They speak in terms of what they *would* do in a given situation instead of giving specific examples of what they *did* do in the past. Generalities are not what we are after.

For example, when asked:

"Tell us about a time you received constructive criticism or feedback. How did you use it to improve your work?"

Candidates often give a vague response like this:

"I think constructive criticism is important. I take the information that someone gives me and apply it to future projects or work that I do. I love for people to let me know how I am doing."

The above response may seem positive and appropriate, but it does not answer the question. Here is an example of an appropriate answer:

"There was one time at Company XYZ when a client called to ask a question. I had to do some research so it took me several days to get back to them. My manager got a call from the client saying that they had not heard back from me to date. My manager told me that I should always touch base with the client within 24 hours of a request even if I do not have the answer. From then on, I have made it a point to return phone calls promptly. If I have to do some research, I will give the client a call within 24 hours and let them know that I have not forgotten about them but still working on getting their question answered. I have since found that clients really appreciate the feedback and knowing that they are still on my mind."

Do you see the differences between Answer #1 and Answer #2? Number 2 actually answered the question.

Employers use the behavioral interview method because it aids in understanding your work style. They have better insight into your decision-making skills and how you learn from your past experiences.

When answering behavioral questions, you should pull from your previous positions. Of course as a senior in college, you may be thinking that you do not have a lot of work history, however, if you do not have a lot of career examples to draw from, then use school or encounters that you have had within other organizations. Provide whatever real-life examples you have. Do not simply answer the question vaguely or with generalities.

Speak clearly...do not mumble, speak loudly, sit up straight

We once interviewed a gentleman who was so soft-spoken that we literally had to lean forward to hear his responses to every question. If he was interviewing for a position where talking would not be a part of his daily job then he may have been a good candidate, however, the role he was seeking was one where he would have to interact with clients every day. I could not imagine having him talk to customers because they would not be able to hear him.

It is extremely important that you show in your interview that you are articulate, that you speak clearly and that you are comfortable talking to people especially if this is part of the job description. Most jobs have some form of people interaction even if it is just with your colleagues.

Never speak negatively about your current or former employer

It is not a good move to dish dirt on your current or former employer. You should have many positive things to say about a previous employer, otherwise you simply come off as being a negative person. Employers do not want to add a negative person to their team. Negativity impacts everyone. It is like a contagious disease. It spreads and can affect employees that have been happy at work until the new pessimistic employee came along. It may not even be a matter of this person encouraging others to be unenthusiastic; a negative person can also simply drain the energy from a room just by entering it. Do not be this person!

Know the appropriate and inappropriate questions to ask during an interview

The interview is the time for a potential employer to ask you questions that will give them insight into your character, work ethic, previous work experience and company knowledge. This is also a time for you to ask questions that will allow you to become more familiar with the company. You should definitely ask questions. It shows that you are genuinely interested in the position and it will give you more information about the opportunity.

We have only had a few candidates that have interviewed with us that have had no questions. This leaves us a bit baffled because although we cover the details of the position well during the interview process, it is difficult to believe that a candidate would not have one question. It leaves us wondering if they are even interested in the position at all.

Your first interview is not the time to ask about money and benefits. Of course your interviewer knows that you are looking for a job and that money is probably a major factor, however, no employer wants to think that money is your primary motivator. We want to know that you are there because you think you can bring something to the table, that you are excited about working for this (and not just any) company and that you want to help our organization grow and prosper. In turn your hard work will be recognized and of course *you* will grow and prosper as well.

Good questions to ask (always ask a question)

The following are examples of good questions to ask your interviewer:

1. What is your vision for the company in the next 3 to 5 years?

2. What makes this company different from its competitors?

3. It seems that you use your website as a marketing tool, what other methods are used to reach your customers?

4. I notice you also have an office in Houston, do you have any additional plans for expansion in the future?

5. What do you think is the key attribute for someone to be successful in this position? At the company?

You want to ask questions that are relevant to the business, that show you have done some research and demonstrate you've put some thought into what the company does.

Don't just ask a question to seem smart or interested. Employers can often see right through this. You want to be genuine and ask questions because you want to know more about the company and the position. You should be excited to be considered for any role you apply to and receive an interview for.

Questions you should never ask

How long have you all been in business?

If this information is on the company website or plastered in the lobby area, this is not a question you want to ask. This shows one of two things—you did not do your research or you are not very observant.

How much does the position pay?

If and when you are offered the position, you will be told about the pay and benefits. Employers know that this is a factor in your decision-making process. You should take the time to evaluate whether or not the pay and benefits are right for you AFTER you are offered the job. We are not saying pay is not important, it is to most people, but you do not want this to appear to be your primary motivator during the interview process.

If you are offered the position, you can request that you be given until the end of the day or the next day to make a decision. You do not want to make a rash decision and decline a position simply because you have in mind a certain amount you would like to make. You also have to take other things into consideration such as how the position will reflect on your résumé and the experiences you will gain from the opportunity.

> I had the opportunity to meet with a very successful gentleman several years ago. He was an entrepreneur and I wanted to know how he did it. I also wanted to know what motivated him and how he figured out what he wanted to do. He told me a story about getting out of college and being offered a position at a firm where he started at $10,000 per year. He knew that he was being underpaid for the responsibilities he was taking on but at the time he knew that he could learn a lot and the experience would ultimately help him accomplish his long-term goals. He stayed at the firm for a few years, learned a great deal and took that knowledge into his own business whereby he became a very successful restaurateur. Had he not taken that initial low-paying job, he may not have been equipped with what he needed to be successful in his own business and become the millionaire he is today. Thus, it is important that you look at the big picture. This means not just evaluating where you are now, but thinking about how today's decisions could impact your future plans. —*Monica*

When will I be considered for a raise?

This creates the same perception we discuss above: It appears as if money is your primary focus.

What type of medical/dental coverage do you all have?

This question may raise a red flag with an employer because they may think you have a health condition that could impede your work or drive up healthcare costs for the firm in the future. Though benefits are important, again let them present this information to you once you have been offered the job. Also, if you are offered the job and the amount of pay or benefits is not mentioned, it is okay to ask at that point. Many companies will provide you with an offer letter that will outline these items as well.

Memorable interview moments:

Memorable Moment #1

> **Interviewer:** Tell me about a time when you had to go above and beyond in your job?
>
> **Answer:** I cannot think of a time where I had to go above and beyond.
>
> **Interviewer:** Really, was there maybe a time you worked late to get a project done or answered a call without being asked?
>
> **Answer:** No, I really cannot think of anything.

Memorable Moment #2

We once had a candidate that made it through the interview process and was offered the position but then requested that we pay her on a weekly basis. We pay our staff bi-weekly which had previously been discussed. This was, in our opinion, an unreasonable request.

Memorable Moment #3

I once had someone call me to follow up on their résumé. I am always very cordial when people call me regarding a job opening. I talked to her for about five minutes. During the conversation she mentioned that she had left her previous job because she had a "nervous breakdown." Of course I am not sure what she was dealing with at that time in her life but what I did know is that the words "nervous breakdown" threw up a red flag in my mind. The job she wanted was fairly intense and deadline-oriented. The last thing I would want is for her to have a reoccurrence of her nervous breakdown. That would not do her or the company any good.

You do not want to say anything to make your employer feel like you will be drama, that you would be more trouble than you are worth. Do not volunteer information that is not asked.

Memorable Moment #4

A phone interview that I had recently went like this: I called a candidate who applied for one position in our company however, I thought she might be a good fit for another position based on her résumé. I called to discuss the other position with her. I explained the job responsibilities and asked if it sounded like something she would be interested in. Her response to me was, "It depends on how much it pays. I have to think about myself; I have bills to pay."

Don't get me wrong I am aware that we all have responsibilities that require money—utilities, car payments, rent or mortgage, but employers are not interested in someone looking for "a job." They want someone interested in the company, position and the team. Employers can hire anyone looking for "a job." Thus, making it so painfully clear that you're all about the money does not go over well with a potential employer. It just proves that you are not truly interested in the company, its growth, mission or vision. People in growing companies do not want these types of people as employees.

Since we are at this point, let's again take a look at what an employer is looking for in a candidate. They want someone who will put the mission of the company first, then put the team second and themselves last.

This may seem counterintuitive because we all have an internal drive to survive and do well, however, you must keep in mind that in order for you to have a job the company has to meet its goals, i.e. its mission. The team works together to reach the mission and you are a part of that team. You, the individual, are a valuable part of accomplishing the overall mission of the company. So expressing that "you have bills to pay" is not the way to get a job.

Memorable Moment #5

I once asked a candidate who had just graduated why he wanted to work for our company. He had literally been out of school for one month. This is how the conversation went:

>**Interviewer:** Why do you want to work here?
>
>**Interviewee:** I think that I can learn a lot about graphic design and the ins and outs of the business.
>
>**Interviewer:** Where do you see yourself in two years?
>
>**Interviewee:** Owning a graphic design company similar to this one along with a t-shirt line.

You may be thinking: what was wrong with that conversation? The problem is that no employer wants to think that your only interest in their company is solely for your own benefit.

Don't get me wrong, I love an entrepreneurial spirit. I celebrate it.

It is an absolutely beautiful thing but this should not be your primary reason for taking a job. An employer does not want to think that as soon as they get you trained, you are going to be out of the door. Training a new employee costs a company a lot of money. It requires that someone actually do the training—a person who could possibly be doing something that produces revenue.

You should be honest if some day you desire to own a business but you do not want to create the perception that you are staying at a company only as long as it will take to get what you need from it. Employers desire to hire people that want to work to grow the company and not just to help themselves. Again, remember the mission → the team → the individual.

The interview is truly your time to shine. Do not take it lightly. Someone has given time out of their busy schedule to get to know you better and in some instances it may be several people. You want to leave them with a lasting, positive impression of you and what you have to offer the company.

6

After the Interview

Send a thank you note

Three days after the interview, you should send the interviewer(s) a personal thank you note. After all, they selected you out of many applicants and they took time out of their busy schedules to talk to you.

Many institutions used to teach that writing a thank you note was part of the job-hunting process. You had your cover letter, résumé and you always followed up with a thank you note after an interview. But today, the thank you note seems to be a lost art. In our experience, only one out of every 10 people that we interview actually follows up with one. You should use this to your advantage because it will make you stand out from the crowd.

The classic way of doing this is to write a handwritten note and put it in the mail. While that would be the most personal and impressive way to express your appreciation, it may take so long to get to the interviewer that the effect would be lost. A thank you email will suffice.

We once interviewed a young man named William. William did well in the phone interview so we called him in for a face-to-face interview and a skills test. He did great in both interviews, but his test results were terrible. William seemed like a great guy but there was no way we could have hired him because he simply lacked the required skills for the job. After each interview, however, William sent us a very thoughtful thank you email.

> Ms. Allen,
>
> I just wanted to say thank you for taking out the time to speak with me yesterday. I really appreciate you all for even considering me as a candidate for the position. You can't imagine how excited I am. I enjoyed speaking with you and look forward to hopefully meeting with you all in the near future.
>
> Again I just wanted to say thank you.
>
> Sincerely, William West

Then after the face-to-face interview, he sent this email:

> Ms. Allen,
>
> It was a pleasure meeting with you and Mr. Allen on Thursday. I just wanted to thank you again for considering me for the position. I look forward to hearing from you.
>
> Sincerely, William West

Just because William was thoughtful enough to follow up with a thank you note, we seriously thought about hiring him for the job. Unfortunately, we could not make it work, but his etiquette really impressed us and made him stand out above all of the other applicants. If William had the necessary skills, we would have definitely hired him.

Always follow every interview with a thank you note. You'd be surprised at what a difference it can make especially when so few people do this anymore.

Follow-up

If you haven't heard back from the employer within a week after your interview, it is perfectly acceptable to send a follow-up email. Your email might sound something like this:

Hi Mr. Smith,

I hope all is well. My name is Carla Jones and I interviewed for the Basket Weaver position last Thursday. I was just wondering if a hiring decision has been made yet. I am still very interested in the job and I know my experience and skill set would be a great asset to the team.

I would love to hear back from you once a decision is made. Thank you again for considering me for the position.

Sincerely, Carla Jones

After about a week, if you don't get a response to your follow-up email, then you can try with a phone call (after all, technology isn't perfect—they may not have received your email). It's not always a good idea to follow up repeatedly, though; somewhere between being persistent and being a pest, there is a field. That field is where you want to be.

I landed my first real job by being persistent. The interview seemed like it went smoothly and I did well on the graphic design skills test. The lady who interviewed me, Melissa, expressed that she thought I would be a good fit for the job. I didn't hear anything for a week, so I decided to call Melissa to see if a decision had been made. She had someone screening her calls so I couldn't speak directly to her but they told me that she would contact me once a decision was made. Melissa called me back and told me that there was another candidate who completed the skills test faster than I did. When I took the test, I was under the impression that I was being assessed more for accuracy than speed, so I told Melissa that I was quite capable of completing the test faster; I was just taking my time to make sure that everything was super-accurate. I offered to come back in and take another test now knowing that speed was top priority. I took the test again and beat the other candidate's completion time by several minutes. Melissa offered me the job on the spot. If I had not been persistent and followed up after the interview, then the other candidate would have won out over me. —E. K. Allen

> I also landed my very first job ever by being persistent. I wanted badly to work at Wal-Mart when I was in high school so I completed an application. I did not hear back for several weeks so one day when I just happened to be in the store, I simply approached the manager and asked him about my application. He stated that they had been trying to reach me. I did not necessarily believe this but I expressed my desire to have an interview. He interviewed me that day and asked me to come back and take their internal test within a couple of days. I was hired by the end of the week. —*Monica*

Always follow up. It not only shows that you are still interested but it keeps you fresh on the interviewer's mind. Plus, your timing may be just right.

A few things to note:

- Never follow up in-person (retail positions can often be an exception to this rule). This can be perceived as rude and threatening. If you weren't chosen for the position, then it would be uncomfortable for someone to have to give you the bad news to your face. It's best not to put people in this awkward situation.

- Don't call or email every day. In fact, if you have followed up two or three times and haven't received a response, just let it go.

In a perfect world, employers would notify every person that interviewed once they have made a hiring decision. Unfortunately, it doesn't always happen like that. Employers usually have multiple candidates that they want to hire, so they will try one person out but they don't tell the other candidates that they were not chosen. Why? Two reasons:

1. If it doesn't work out with Candidate A, then the employer can go back and hire Candidate B without Candidate B knowing that he was really the second choice.

2. Most people aren't comfortable with confrontation. It's not easy to be the bearer of bad news and tell someone that they weren't chosen for the job.

So if you don't hear back after an interview, don't get discouraged! Keep in mind that some companies will do several interviews prior to making a hiring decision. We have found the more times you interview someone, the better you get to know them. We even occasionally have someone come in and meet with the entire team or work around the office for a few hours as part of the consideration process. It is important that you do not take these opportunities lightly.

7

The Offer

What to Expect

So you've followed all of the advice, shined in your interviews and followed up properly. A job offer could be extended to you at any minute. Be prepared.

Although it rarely happens, you could get an offer during an interview. More often, an employer will call you and/or email you a few days after the interview and present you with a job offer.

At a minimum, the offer should outline the following things:

- your position
- your pay
- the frequency of pay
- your schedule
- your start date

These details may first be presented to you verbally then once you have accepted, they should be presented to you in writing.

Negotiating salary

Many sources will tell you to never accept the first salary offer and to negotiate higher pay. We, however, would advise strongly against this, especially in these economic times. We have witnessed too many situations where a candidate shot themselves in the foot by trying to negotiate a higher pay without having any leverage.

Imagine a conversation like this:

> Hiring Manager (HM): ...and based on your experience, your starting salary would be $30,000 a year.
> Job Applicant (JA): *Is the salary negotiable?*
> HM: *Well what do you propose?*
> JA: *I was hoping for at least $35,000 a year.*
> HM: *Well this position pays $30,000 for someone with your level of experience. If you are saying that the company should pay you more, what more do you have to offer?*
> JA: _____

(You fill in the above blank with how you would answer this question.)

Here are some examples of what *not* to say:

> "Well, I need X amount of dollars to support my lifestyle."
> "Because I know that I'll do great at this job."
> "I don't know, I just thought I would try to ask for more."

Obviously, none of these are good answers. There really isn't a good answer unless you have *leverage*. This means that you must have something to offer that is quantifiably *above and beyond* the normal job requirements so that the employer can justify paying you *above and beyond* the normal starting salary.

So what's an example of a good reason to justify asking for a higher salary? Only an answer like this would make sense:

> "Well, according to my research, most companies pay $35,000-$40,000 a year for someone in this field with my level of experience. I actually have another offer from XYZ Company for $35,000 for the same job so I hope you understand that I'll have to weigh all of my options and get back to you."

In a scenario like this, a) everything you are saying better be true and b) you had better be able to prove that you are worth every penny and more.

In most cases, trying to negotiate salary is an all-around bad move. Companies want employees that are customer-centric, team-centric and company mission-centric. Asking for higher pay without any valid justification just makes you look self-centered and money-focused. I have even heard stories of hiring managers rescinding a job offer because the applicant asked for higher pay. Also, keep in mind that companies usually have budgets that they must stick to when making a hiring decision and in this economy there are probably several other candidates who would be happy with the pay offered. It is best to just get in the door and work up from there.

> When I received my first job, I knew that the offer was lower than industry standards for my entry level position, however, I liked the company and I needed a job. There were no other offers on the table, so I took it. I proved my value and within 6 months got an above-average raise. —*Monica*

Thinking it over

If you have a couple of offers on the table or just need some time, it is fine to ask that you have an opportunity to think it over. You want to make sure you get back in touch with your contact person on the day and by the time you stated that you would let them know your decision. Keep in mind that they probably have other interested candidates. They may also be on a timeline for making a decision on getting someone placed in the position.

Getting that first offer is an exciting time. Accept with a thank you and let the person know that you are excited about what you can do for the company and that you cannot wait to get started.

8

Your First Day

You have gone through the process it takes to land the job you want and now it is time for work on your first day. There are a few things you should keep in mind about day one of employment.

You are still interviewing

You should approach your first day of employment as if you are still on an interview. Your manager is still observing your behavior to assure themselves that they made the right decision and chose the best candidate for the position. Also keep in mind that many companies have a probationary period. You should do the following to prepare:

- **Get a good night's rest.** You do not want to arrive on your new job exhausted. It does not look good to be yawning as your manager shows you around or gets you started on your new duties does. Also, depending on your new job, if you are tired, you could easily fall asleep sitting for a long period of time. The last thing you want is for your new boss to catch you snoozing on the first day (or any day for that matter).

- **Arrive on time.** If you came to your interview during the late morning or early afternoon, traffic may be very different during Monday morning rush hour, thus you need to plan accordingly. Leave extra early. Do not run the risk of arriving to work late on your first day. If you have enough time between acceptance of the position and your start date, do a couple of trial runs getting from your home to the office during the time of day you would be expected to arrive. Know an alternate route just in case you run into traffic and need to detour. Arriving to work late on your very first day is not how you want to start your new employment relationship.

- **Arrive as well-groomed the first day as you did during the interview process.** Now is not the time to rest on your laurels and run out of the house looking sloppy. Dress as sharply as you can without being over-dressed for the job. For example, if you wore a suit to the interview and your daily duties do not require such elaborate dress, then wear the appropriate attire. Whatever the case, you should still be neat and well-groomed.

We once interviewed a young lady we will call Fashion Faux-Pas Felicia. She arrived at both interviews very well put together; her appearance was top notch and she was very stylish. Since she was going to be working in our high-end retail clothing store, we thought that her impeccable sense of style combined with her management experience would make her a good fit for the job, so we hired her.

Not long after starting the position, however, Felicia's sense of style went downhill. The trendy pants and blouses were replaced with leggings and belted cotton tops. Felicia must have pulled out her best two outfits for the interviews and this gave us a false sense of her fashion capabilities. It seemed like everything in her closet was too casual, too athletic and/or too inappropriate to wear while interacting with customers in our upscale boutique. —*Monica*

Here are a few other things that you should be prepared to do on your first day of employment:

Come prepared to complete your legal paperwork

It is very helpful to the Human Resources department if you come prepared to complete your legal paperwork. This includes your W-4, State tax forms and I-9. Bring a copy of your passport (if applicable), driver's license and social security card. These will be needed for appropriate record-keeping and reporting purposes. Having these items on the first day will allow this process to be completed quickly and easily. This also means the Human Resources manager or owner will not have to harass you for it later. In addition, you will not have to remember to bring it in the next day and thus look forgetful or like a slacker if you do not remember.

You should take notes

Most of us would like to think that we have these extraordinary brains that will remember everything, but on your first day of employment you will probably be given a lot of information. In addition, you will be excited, your adrenaline will be pumping, and you may even be a little nervous, so you probably will not remember everything. In a large office building, you may even forget your way to the restroom.

Taking notes on your first day and throughout your tenure has strong advantages. This shows you are paying attention and that you are interested in what is being said or taught. When taking notes you do not have to write down every single word your manager says, however, you want to take down the important information. For example, if you have daily duties that you are being trained on, taking notes will enable you to do them effectively on your second day without continually having to ask questions. This is very impressive because most managers and executives hate having to repeat themselves. Taking notes shows initiative and will give the impression that you are extremely smart and competent. Remember that your manager or trainer has a lot on her plate so having to repeat something she has already said may annoy her. Taking notes can help avoid this and it will demonstrate that you are on top of things from day one.

When I entered Corporate America right out of college, there were two things I made a habit of doing. The first was taking notes in meetings. Not only did this allow me to go back and review something later, but it also gave me an opportunity to jot down questions that I may have wanted to ask when the time was appropriate.

The second thing I did was create a dedicated notebook for important information I needed to know for my job. Since I worked in the insurance industry, I took detailed notes on various types of insurance policies. Once I learned the appropriate formulas for calculating certain premiums accurately, I would write the formulas in my notebook as well. This allowed me to refer to my notes rather than continuing to ask my manager how to do it. In addition, it helped me learn things a lot faster because I could study my notes on my own time. —*Monica*

When we started our own company, we thought that taking notes in a meeting was common practice. Boy, were we wrong. We have seen people in meetings doodling, staring off into space or just nodding their head at every word. For the most part, our entire staff does not take notes but the employees that do happen to be the same ones who excel in everything they do. Is that just a coincidence? We do not think so.

The first day of your new job will be exciting and maybe even a little bit nerve-racking but being prepared will help calm you and reassure your employer about their hiring decision.

9

No one owes you anything

We currently live in a time where immediate gratification is expected. Many people lack patience and feel like they are owed something just for being present. We are all unique in our own way but no matter how special you are, you still have to work for the desired result. Just showing up does not cut it so get ready to grind if you want to be successful. Upon entering the work force, it is very important that you are realistic, diligent, proactive and patient. You are not going to be offered the position of CEO after being at the company for a week. You will also probably not make the kind of money you thought you would, coming right out of school.

> I once worked with a young man whom we will call Over-Ambitious Andy. Ambition is usually a good thing but Andy's ambitions eventually lead to his getting laid off when the company hit a rough patch. Starting with the company right out of school, Andy was very eager to learn (which of course we all thought was great) but after about 6 months we could sense his discontent. Andy wanted to be promoted but his manager thought he still had a lot to learn. Andy needed more time and experience on the job.

He was neither mature nor knowledgeable enough to face clients and to confidently discuss the products. He felt like he was being held back. I tried to encourage Andy by letting him know that I was once in his shoes. Before I moved up the corporate ladder, I remained in an entry level position for almost 2 years because I had a lot to learn. I shared with Andy that I remained patient and eventually I moved up fairly quickly, however, my advice was not something Over-Ambitious Andy wanted hear. He became unhappy and a little disgruntled. His manager sensed his frustration and encouraged him to hang in there and continue to learn. When word came down that every department had to lay off some people to cut costs, Andy was one of the first people to go. Our manager felt that Andy wasn't happy anyway. No one wants to be around unhappy, negative people for one-third of their day.—*Monica*

When you get out of school it is important you're aware that college did not prepare you for your actual job. You were taught some basics with your major and if you think about it, you only take a handful of classes that are directly related to your subject of focus. You're required to take the other classes to ensure you have a well-balanced experience. When you actually go to work for a company, you will have many things to learn. Don't act like a know-it-all because you really know nothing at all. You will have to be taught about the industry, the particular firm that you are working for and how that business is run from day-to-day. If you are able to get a job directly related to your major, you may have some basic knowledge of the most generally-accepted concepts, but studying something in school is not the same as actually practicing it every day for customers and clients. Thus, it is extremely important that you come into your company with an eagerness to learn. You must be patient and realize that you will not be the President or CEO in a year or two, but people will acknowledge your enthusiasm. They will value that you have the ability to get your job done effectively and efficiently. If you are working for a good firm, those attributes will be noted and rewarded. The incentive may not come in the package or timing you feel you deserve, but it will come. Keep in mind that executives are focused on the bigger picture for the company—a perspective you have not yet developed. They know the skills and knowledge needed at the next level. They also know what the organization requires now and what will be necessary for it to be successful in the future. It is vitally important that if you enjoy your job you do not become impatient for what may eventually come.

Now you may be asking, "What if I feel like I have not been treated fairly or I have been passed over for a promotion? What should I do?"

If you have been in a company for a couple of years and have not received the promotion that you thought you should have gotten, or you have been passed over for individuals with less tenure, then you should speak to your manager rationally and calmly. Ask him or her what you need to do to be considered for the next level. Discuss what additional skills you need to acquire to be viable for promotion. The hope is that your company, whether big or small, has done effective performance reviews on an ongoing basis so nothing you discuss with your manager will be a shock. Now of course, in order for you to be regarded as someone ready for additional responsibility, you need to do the things that were discussed between you and your manager. Also, watch those individuals who are getting promoted. How do they seem to work differently from you? Do they meet deadlines while you miss yours by a day or two? Do you always have a "good" excuse for missing your deadlines? Do they arrive early and/or stay late? Be honest with yourself. Do not look at your performance through rose-colored glasses. We all have areas that we can improve upon. What are yours?

Take a moment to fill out the Self Evaluation form on the next page. Be sure to answer everything honestly, then total up your score.

Self-Evaluation Form

	Above Average 5 Points	Average 3 Points	Below Average 0 Points
I arrive to work on time			
I use my time productively			
I am proficient with the required tools to complete my work product			
I work well with other employees			
I meet task deadlines			
I am enthusiastic about my work			
I put forth my best effort			
I am able to cope with changes			
I am able to work without constant supervision			
I take responsibility for my decisions and actions			
When I provide feedback it is constructive			
I follow company rules and policies			
I refrain from handling personal affairs on company time			
Total			

Score:

Less than 39 = Major Room for Improvement

39-45 = Room for Improvement

39-65 = Very Good

65 = Do it Again (BE HONEST) No one is perfect.

How did you do? Were you honest with yourself? Did you discover some areas you need to work on? If so, more than likely, your manager has noticed them too. Begin to work on these things so nothing will hold you back from accomplishing your goals and realizing your full potential.

10

Get an Unpaid Internship

At this point you may have followed all of the steps in this book but you have yet to land a job. What do you do? We suggest that you find a company that you would like to work for in your field of interest and ask someone if you could come on as an unpaid intern. A company may not be in a financial position to hire you but would welcome an extra set of hands and the opportunity to develop a college graduate.

No pay?

You may be thinking NO PAY…what is up with that? Are you serious?! Look at it this way: You do not have a job so an unpaid internship will allow you to stay busy and gain skills and experiences that will enhance your résumé.

There are some schools that strongly encourage obtaining an internship during your matriculation. Some offer college credits or make it a pre-requisite for graduation. Some of these opportunities may be paid or unpaid; it depends on the college's requirements. Either way, this is a great opportunity to network, gain experience and get to know the industry. It allows you to truly work in the field and not just study about it in a classroom.

Even if your school does not require or encourage you to get an internship, get one any way, especially if you are a recent graduate and have not yet found a job. This is a way to get your foot in the door. Multi-millionaire music mogul Sean "Puffy/P. Diddy/Diddy" Combs started as an intern at Uptown Records. His position was the catalyst that ultimately led to his success in the music industry.

> As a college student, I decided that I wanted to change my major from engineering. I was not quite sure what I wanted to do, but I knew it was no longer engineering. Since I started considering the business school, more specifically the Risk Management and Insurance program, I went to my family's insurance agent, Robert Service, and asked him if I could work there during the Christmas holidays. I wanted to see what the day-to-day work was like and if it seemed like something I would enjoy. Mr. Service said "yes" without hesitation and this was very helpful to me.
>
> A year or so later after changing my major to Risk Management and Insurance, I obtained an internship in the Worker's Compensation department of a very large insurance firm. Fortunately this was a paid internship and the knowledge I gained and the real life experience was truly priceless. It looked great on my résumé that I had worked for just a few months in a professional environment and I had a manager that gladly gave me stellar recommendations. —*Monica*

What do I do as an intern?

When you get your position as an intern you want to work for the company as if you are getting paid every day. Do not take this opportunity lightly. You do what is asked in a timely manner and with enthusiasm. If you are genuinely interested in the company and the field, this will be apparent to everyone around you. They will ultimately hate to lose you, your energy and your enthusiasm for the company. Even if they are unable to hire you full-time, you will have gained some connections in the industry as well as some great references. Your manager will be able to tell a future employer how invaluable you are and how well you were able to demonstrate a strong work ethic each day.

Don't be afraid to make your mark

We have had several interns at our company over the years, both paid and unpaid. They are included in staff meetings and learn various areas of the business. Our interns have never been afraid to make suggestions or recommendations. As a new set of eyes, you may notice something that can be completed more efficiently that management may have missed because they are "in it" every day. Keep in mind though that you are there to learn, so if the team does not implement your suggestion it may be that it has been tried before or it just isn't feasible. Do not get discouraged. Be a sponge. Learn all that you can and enthusiastically contribute as well.

The new economy

To gain a job in this new economy, it is vitally important that you are as polished as you can be in every way possible. You must stand out from the crowd. From the very beginning, you must put your best foot forward. Your résumé should be top-notch. Your approach at a career fair should be professional and it never hurts to practice your interview skills.

Having had the opportunity to interview many students coming right out of school, we know there is work to be done. You want to be well-written and well-spoken. None of us are perfect so fine-tune your job-seeking abilities. If necessary, read this book again. Make sure you are the cream of the crop. We wish you the best. Learn more and keep in touch with us at www.now-what-books.com.

www.ingramcontent.com/pod-product-compliance
Lightning Source LLC
Chambersburg PA
CBHW071630040426
42452CB00009B/1563